Echoes
From My Heart

Poems by
Jo Ann Jones

Echoes
From My Heart

Poems By
Jo Ann Jones

Published By
Positive Imaging, LLC
http://positive-imaging.com
bill@positive-imaging.com

Cover designed by A. William Benitez
and Rebecca Hoeft

All rights reserved. No part of this book may be reproduced, transmitted or downloaded in any form or by any means, electronic or mechanical, including copying, photocopying, recording or by any information storage and retrieval system without written permission from the author, except for the inclusion of brief quotations in a review.

Copyright   2016   Jo Ann Jones
ISBN   9781944071103

Scriptures noted are taken from The Holy Bible
New International Version c1978
by New York International Bible Society

A Guide For Living

Dedication	**11**
Acknowledgment	**13**
Introduction	**15**
Faith	**17**
He Is Always Near	*19*
Restored Faith	*20*
Victory	*21*
Armor of God	*22*
Christ's Family	*23*
Our Prayer	*24*
He Calms the Storms	*25*
Would You Walk On Water	*26*
Enjoy Each Day	*27*
Life's Book	*28*
True Faith	*29*
His Disciples	*30*
A New Perspective	*32*
Witnessing	**33**
Just One	*35*
All Things Work For Good	*36*
Love One Another	*37*
Be His Witness	*38*
Don't Settle For Less	*39*
Our Task	*40*
Praise Him	*41*
Road Pavers	*42*
God Is In Control	*43*
The Demons	*44*

The Day of Judgment	45
A Mission Encounter	46
Show Me	47
My Role	48
Front Row Disciples	49
God's Super Bowl	50

Devotion — 51

A Second Wedding	53
Our Bridegroom	54
The Race	55
Our Devotion	56
The Star of the Show	57
Marriage Is God's Masterpiece	58
Empathy	59
Friendship	60
Servile Master	61
His Name	62
Transcending Love	63

Forgiveness — 65

Christ's Invitation	67
My Life's Story	68
Christ's Banquet	69
With Nothing	70
Set Your Course	71
Forgiveness	72

Dependence — 73

Your Choice	75
The Battle	76
Control Released	77

List Your Blessings	78
The Storms of Life	79
Who Moved?	80
Jesus Has Been There	81
He Waits	82
Road of Life	83
Last Days	84
The Good Shepard	85
What If, Lord?	86

Listening   87

Whisper His Name	89
Why Me?	90
Worry Not	91
Our Future	92
Self Inventory	93
Shared Whispers	94
Our Shepherd	95
Night of Wonder	96
Who Knew?	97
Thoughts Shared	98
Time For New Wine	100

Memories   101

Fighting for Freedom	103
Broken Vessels	104
My Father	105
Our Daughter	106
Our Sixtieth Anniversary	107
Goodbye, My Love	108
Two Minus One	109
The Columbia Tragedy	110

Humor 111

Birthday Nightmare	*113*
Good Morning	*114*
Too Much Stuff	*115*
My Epitaph	*116*
The Aging Game	*117*
Forever Young	*118*
A High School Reunion	*119*
Calling All Worrywarts	*120*
Mature Love	*121*
What's Your Name	*122*
Insomnia	*123*
Ring-a-Dingy	*124*
Politics	*125*
Too Young To Be This Old	*126*
Vanity's Woes	*127*
Patience Wins	*128*
Eternal Youth	*129*
Not Ms America	*130*
Over the Hill Blues	*131*
Senior Moments	*132*
Her Silent Love	*133*
My Second Childhood	*134*
Long Living Rats	*135*
The Mature Youth	*136*
Not For Lunch	*137*
Our 60th Reunion	*138*
The Good Ole Days	*139*
The Welcoming Committee	*140*
The Parent Trap	*142*

Holiday   145

    A New Year   147
    Resolutions   148
    New Opportunities   149
    True Love   150
    Forty Days   151
    God's Plan   152
    Deny Him Not   153
    The Shouts   154
    After Easter   156
    Resurrection Proclaimed   157
    Salute To Moms   158
    Memorial Day   159
    Father of All Fathers   160
    Thanksgiving   161
    Giving Thanks   162
    Son of God   163
    There Is Room   164
    In Our Midst   165
    God's Christmas Gift   166
    A Holy Event   167
    Affluenza   168
    Would We?   169
    God's Holy Heir   170
    Christmas Each Day   172
    What Is Christmas?   173
    Two Views of Christmas   174

About Jo Ann Jones   175

DEDICATION

This book of poems is lovingly dedicated to my deceased husband, James W. Jones, the love of my life for 60 years. When I first began writing poems, he constantly provided me support. His encouragement supplied the confidence to believe in myself and to continue writing.

Jimmy was an amazing Christian; devoted to his Savior and Lord. Over his lifespan, he daily lived out the essence of each poem and its truths. I praise God for blessing me with a husband who knew, expressed and shared such abiding love. I miss him greatly and await our reunion.

ACKNOWLEDGMENT

My deepest appreciation to my friends Katherine Brown and Becky Hoeft for their support and enthusiasm. They generously volunteered many hours of their time and were always available whatever the need. As we worked together we shared ideas, suggestions and much laughter resulting in a deeper friendship. From the very beginning their belief in this project further strengthened my confidence.

I offer my deepest gratitude to Bill Benitez of Positive Imaging, LLC. As a novice I had no knowledge about book publishing. Bill patiently guided me step by step from the original concept to the end. I received his counsel and expert advice and appreciated his insightful suggestions. Without Bill's professional assistance this book would not have been published.

*"Whatever you do, work at it with all your heart,
as working for the Lord, not for men"
Colossians 3:23*

INTRODUCTION

Poetry is painting that speaks
Painting is silent poetry

Echoes From My Heart is a compilation of poems I have been writing for many years. It's a collection of poems inspired throughout my life's challenges and joys. My family and friends offered continuous inspiration and encouragement.

Thank you for purchasing this book, and I hope it touched you in some way. The poems are divided into nine topics, so you can choose to read the poems in any order. Each topic page has a scripture to share God's word for the upcoming poems. Read these poems at your leisure or when you need a reminder of God's blessings and grace.

I'd like to share another 'Echo' with you. After the costs of publishing and distribution are met, the remaining profit of my book will be donated to the Florida United Methodist Children's Home in Deltona, FL.

I pray that when my life is over and every bit of my talent gone, that I say to God, "I used up everything you gave me."

FAITH

*Let us fix our eyes on Jesus, the
author and perfecter of our faith…*

Hebrews12:2a

He Is Always Near

At times in the midst of problems
Of God's presence we're not aware
Our mind is filled with worldly things
But solutions won't be found there.

Feeling frightened and alone
We look heavenward and cry out
"Lord, where in the world are you?"
Voices filled with disparaging doubt.

Immediately we hear his reply
"I never left; I stayed right here
And while we're on this subject
Where and why did you disappear?"

Our balance of life is restored
Now our burdens on Him we cast
Vowing in His presence to stay
Knowing Christ's promises hold fast.

Restored Faith

How easy it is to keep the faith
When all is running our way
But the true test comes when all is flawed
And despair and defeat crowd our day.

We battle against sin's depression
Which saps our strength and our will
We're rendered impotent and beaten
Till His voice fills the night so still.

The solution is really so simple
Speak His name softly in prayer
He's there beside you instantly
Erasing your worry and care.

Life is still rugged but faith is restored
We resume our journey in peace
Wrapped up in Christ's mantle of love
As to Him each day we release.

Victory

God is in His heaven
But, not all is right with the world
Its prince is wily Satan
Whose sins about us swirl.

Christ is in the world, not of it
When Satan tempted Jesus thrice
Jesus Christ rebuked the devil
When on the cross He paid our price.

Many trials and troubles come
Read the newspaper; hear the news
We run around in circles
While all about us unglues.

Some think with wealth and power
The world will soon be theirs
We're shocked by horrific events
But know that Jesus still cares.

To gain the world, but lose our souls
How foolish that would be
For Christ takes our doom and gloom
And turns them into victory.

Armor of God

We are not defenseless against evil
God enables us to stand firm
He girds us with His full armor
To fight sin… Satan's germ.

We buckle on the belt of truth
And speak in love to one another
Put on the breastplate of righteousness
Showing concern for each other.

With faith's shield we can resist Satan
And Christ's helmet proclaims salvation
The sword of the Spirit is God's Word
Providing us with faith and inspiration.

Pray constantly for all God's saints
Always mindful of Satan's wiles
Battle injustice and suffering
While the lost, Jesus reconciles.

When we don the whole armor of God
His presence strengthens and sustains
With praise and reverence rely on His power
For yesterday, today, forever God reigns.

Christ's Family

Before we became
Children of God
We were prisoners of Satan's mind
We followed the way
Of this lurid world
And were sinful, selfish, unkind.

We labored to win
Approval from those
Who daily crossed our path
Those much like us
Awaiting judgment
Christ's forgiveness not yet hath.

No matter how good
And saintly we lived
We were still outside Christ's door
Until we entered
And fell on our knees
"Christ forgive my sins," we'd implore.

Through his mercy and grace
The blood Christ shed
We were saved from sin, set free
How great His love
He shares with us all
Who abide in Christ's holy family.

Our Prayer

We pray, "Thy kingdom come, Lord,
On earth as it is in Heaven."
But if this is to come to pass
We each must be the leaven
Used to raise the Bread of Life
Add flavor and substance too
This is our God-given mission
Letting the Master's love shine through.

"Give us this day our daily bread,"
Just necessities, Lord, not a lot
Only you know what's truly needed
Make us satisfied with what we've got
Lord, "Forgive us as we forgive
The trespasses of our brother."
For only in so doing this
Are we able to love one another.

"Lead us not into temptation
Deliver us from evil, Lord."
Help us be strong and faithful
As we cover ourselves with the Word.
"For thine is the kingdom forever,"
Which means we will have eternal life
What great promises you've given us
No more sorrow, pain or strife.

He Calms the Storms

Have you ever been caught in a storm
With claps of thunder and lightning
The angry wind, the rain so cold
Its force and fury so frightening?

While nature's forces can destroy
Christ commands the wind and wave
He opens out His arms to us
And provides the safety we crave.

Troubles are rife about us
We have no strength to go on
Our bodies racked by aches and pain
But Jesus Christ is our balm.

Exhausted, fearful and weakened
Suddenly, so clear is our mind
Christ is the ruler of the universe
And embraces us with a love divine.

Though life's storms still come and go
I know now Christ walks beside me
He calms me with His "Peace…Be still"
And with agape love He ever guides me.

Would You Walk On Water?

If Christ asked you to walk on water
Like Peter would you step out of the boat?
    Ignoring the waves and tides
    Watching Him only as He guides
Over treacherous seas, trying to float.

In trust you confidently take the first step
Still as dry as when you first began.
    Self-assurance your ego swells
    Forgetting in whom the power dwells
And you foolishly let go of Christ's hand.

I can do this by myself, you think
But afraid, quickly sink into the sea.
    Cold water your senses stun
    Seeking safety but finding none
Now forgetting that your only rock is He.

If your doubt takes over, all is lost
The fiercest storms Jesus can calm.
    Angry waves His will obey
    Safe with Him you'll stay
Then Christ will heal us with His balm.

We each must stay focused on our Lord
And ignore everything that us surrounds.
    Abandon self, surrender all
    Respond gladly to Christ's call
Then we can walk on water - homebound.

Enjoy Each Day

Don't take life so seriously
Celebrate each day as it arrives
Your time is up you'll have to go
No matter how hard you strive.

If there are things you wanted
But somehow you never got
Now is the time to acquire them
As this may be your last shot.

If the things you dreamed you'd do
Were delayed; opportunities slid by
Today's the time you 'get up to bat'
So step up and make that ball fly.

Enjoy each day to its fullest
For it's later than you think
Things not done may remain undone
For life can end in one eye's blink.

Don't take anything for granted
Life, friends, loved ones, blessings
Realize how fortunate you are
And your life begin assessing.

For we pass this way but once
And affect those we meet on the way
So live each day as if it's your last
And your witness convey.

Life's Book

How quickly the pages of life are turned
Much like an engrossing book
Plots and subplots scattered within
With characters…both saint and rook.

Each person develops the story
Similar to those we meet on our way
Some cause strife; some bring happiness
The plot changes from day to day.

What's expected doesn't always happen
The unexpected sometimes occurs
But the focus is on the main character
And a happy ending the reader prefers.

Isn't this similar to our lives
Sadness and happiness shares the bill
Foes deflate while friends lift us
A constant struggle to climb the next hill?

Though we do good, we reap injustice
If the world were fair this wouldn't be
But if we emulate the main character
Our complicated lives He can free.

This character, of course, is Jesus
With Him this book never ends
And we will know the future's outlook
If the right message our book sends.

True Faith

Mark tells us about four men
Whose friend was paralyzed
Wanting Christ to heal him
A bold plan they devised.

They carried their friend on a mat
To the house where Christ was teaching
But because of the large crowd there
They knew Jesus they'd not be reaching.

So they climbed upon the rooftop
Through a hole they lowered their friend
Christ, moved by their faith and trust
Brought the man's illness to an end.

Jesus, the Great Physician
Can heal heart, soul and mind
Many others come seeking
Your life, too, He can redesign.

Whatever your need, ask in faith
To Christ, blessed Savior and King
Confess, repent, claim Him as Lord
You'll no longer feel death's sting.

For He has bought you, paid the price
Now with Him you'll share heaven's glory
Till then go and spread the good news
And witness Christ's wondrous story.

His Disciples

When Jesus called his disciples
Ordinary men He chose
With many faults and foibles
Why them… only God knows.

Leaving their jobs and families
They listened as Jesus taught
But knew not the scope of his mission
Nor why to earth Christ was brought.

An earthly kingdom the twelve envisioned
They quarreled who would sit at Christ's side
"The greatest would be but a servant,"
Hearing this their worldly hopes died.

After Christ's death and resurrection
They become the men God did foresee
Spreading the good news around the world
And now with Him share eternity.

Still today this process remains
Through the ages many have heard this call
And they are all merely duplicates
Of the twelve who did stumble and stall.

Seek out your characteristics
Which match those fishers of men.
Regardless of your past or present
You'll not stay as you have been.

Some of us are much like Peter
Impatient, impetuous, bold
We take action before we think
And put our intellect on hold.

Others may resemble Thomas
Needing proof before they believe
Accepting nothing by faith nor trust
Caring not Christ's heart, they grieve.

Many are likened to Matthew
Coveting more wealth, always greedy
Laying up treasures for themselves
Not concerned with the plight of the needy.

Finally, there are those like Judas
Promoting an agenda of their own
Betraying Jesus for a small sum
An act only Satan would condone.

Like us, none of the twelve were perfect
But God is our divine Creator
If we die to 'self' and let him lead
He will forever be our advocator.

So respond to Jesus' challenge
And as his disciple take the high road
And you will live an abundant life
If always Christ you have followed.

A New Perspective

In this world take nothing for granted
Except the new dawn every day
Each blessing in life is but a gift
And can quickly be snatched away.

By rote we go about our routines
Our job, our families, our friends
Activities and hobbies we enjoy
Assuming nothing in life ever ends.

Until the loss of a loved one,
An encounter with some disease
Or loss of financial stability
Each can bring us to our knees.

CHRIST… the same today… forever
Though life about us changes and shifts
When we're in the depths of despair
Our Spirit His mighty power lifts.

He puts our lives in perspective
Such a short time our tour on earth
Though health and fame may be fleeting
He offers a future of infinite worth.

Till then cast all your cares on Him
Savor what each day might bring
You'll be equal to any task
As an adopted child of the King.

You'll see life through different eyes
Expressing love, thankfulness and praise
Enduring whatever comes your way
Because you know there'll be better days.

WITNESSING

You will be his witness to all men of what you have seen and heard.

Acts 22:15

Just One

I am just one person
What can only one mortal do?
But if Christ's love is shared
One could increase to two.

If two Christians witnessed
Their number might grow to four,
And if repeated again and again
It could bring many, many more.

Christianity has spread
For over two thousand years,
One convert winning another
Who will gladly volunteer?

So don't discount your worth
If serving Christ is your mission,
For He will gladly share with you
The heaven on earth He envisions.

All Things Work For Good

All things work together for good
Difficult words for today's world
Rampart sins, wars, pestilence
By Satan and his minions are hurled.

As an angel, Satan was flung from heaven
For God's power he wished to replace
Forgetting that God's Son, Jesus Christ
Died on a cross to save the human race.

Who can dismiss this powerful love
The sacrifice made without measure
Given to us when we claim Christ as Lord
Eternal Life with Him…what a treasure.

Doubt not the promises of Christ
For each of us, God has made a plan
Prayerfully consider and make a choice
That's open to every woman and man.

Love One Another

You can say, "Love one another"
A thousand times or more
But unless action follows speech
Things remain as they were before.

A picture is worth a thousand words
This worldly saying is truly succinct
It separates saints from hypocrites
Who wish only to lip synch.

The Lord has issued His mandate
His love with all we should share
Thus witnessing with a well lived life
As befitting one of Jesus' heirs.

So if you say it, mean it
"Put your shoulder to the plow"
And offer sincere compassion
No pose of 'holier-than-thou'.

We're rowing in the same direction
As sinners who by Christ are redeemed
For He took our place at Calvary
And died, arose, the Victor Supreme.

Be His Witness

We so easily share our thoughts
Relate joys and cares to each other
We talk about TV, movies, sports
Even speculate about the weather.

But when it comes to sharing Christ
Suddenly, so silent we remain
Afraid to voice that we are His
And for our sins, He was slain.

If someone hadn't shared with us
Unsaved we might still be
Without Christ's steadfast promises
That as His child, we'd be set free.

So why not share Christ as a gift
To family, neighbor, co-worker, friend
State His case…then let them choose
For their lives, too, He can mend.

If each of us witnessed to one
This world would be made anew
All because they shared their Christ
Like someone shared Him with you.

Don't Settle For Less

I try to maintain the status quo
But Christ leads me to higher ground
For the evidence of my daily living
Will determine if I'm Heaven bound.

Being human, I try to settle
For less than the Savior would give
And I sadly choose to ignore
The way Christ would have me live.

But once more and then again
He persistently seeks me out
Wanting only the best for me
Not days of despair and doubt.

To live a triumphant life for Him
Will assure satisfaction and peace
With Christ's caring presence near
Souls can take on a new lease.

So don't settle for the temporal
For that's what the world dispenses
Inherit the Kingdom prepared for you
And enjoy His endless consequences.

Our Task

Lord, what have you planned for us
Is it a mission divine?
Something important, earthshaking
Tell us; our task define.

You said Judea, Samaria
And to the uttermost parts
You commanded us to go
And witness to people's hearts.

To sense their spiritual emptiness
And share with them love and grace
That led you up to Calvary
To die on a cross in their place.

We can't believe what you're saying
Judea – stay right where we are
To tell family, neighbors and friends
Christ can remove each stain and scar.

But it's difficult to witness
To those who know us well
They've seen our flaws and defects
And the Truth, they may dispel.

But this is our God-given task
So to your command we succumb
And with our hands in yours, Lord
Watch out Judea…here we come!

Praise Him

God created each of us unique
With our own personalities and gifts
With a soul and will to choose
If praises to Him we will lift.

Some folk praise God through music
With angelic moving voices they sing
Others play various instruments
Each note dedicated to the King.

Emulating Christ while here on earth
Others offer their praise through deeds
By helping those heavy laden and weak
Fulfilling whatever their needs.

Many praise God by sharing His Words
To a world misguided and lost
Who are focused on material things
Unaware for them Christ died on a cross.

I chose to praise God with verse
Using the gift He bestowed on me
And as I share the lessons I've learned
I pray some will accept His guarantee.

No manner of praise is foremost
God finds pleasure in them all
So offer your sincere praises to Him
When you answer His fervent call.

Road Pavers

Many still are searching
For truths they can believe
The world has disappointed
No hope did they receive.

So they wandered aimlessly
To and fro, with no direction
Until they met that someone
Who shared Christ's resurrection.

Their lives turned upside down
With joy and jubilation
For they were now members
Of Christ's New Creation.

Was it you or me they met
That told the Good News story?
For them, Christ lovingly gave His life
So they could live with Him in glory.

Or were we silent bystanders
While others witnessed for Him
Seeing lives transformed, made new
Which minutes before were dim?

We have Christ's marching orders
"Go forth, the world to save"
What greater gift can we offer Him
When the road to Christ we pave?

God Is In Control

When I gave my heart to Jesus
I thought my battles were won
Not realizing that Satan
With me still wasn't done.

Satan increased my struggle
Trying to revert me to his side
Temptations all about me
He wants my bond with God untied.

The devil undermines with doubt
Instilling anxiety and despair
But he still cannot conquer
God's endless love and care.

As promised, Christ didn't forsake me
I'd not face my trials alone
He strengthened and encouraged
As on me his mercies shone.

So when you're feeling tempted
Like each and every day
Wisely turn to the Savior
Only he can keep Satan at bay.

You'll learn not to rely on yourself
For that is courting disaster
Only our Mighty God is in control
So keep your eyes on the Master.

The Demons

Saved, I thought my demons were gone
Today, up popped another one
It was ready and willing to cancel out
The service for Jesus I've done.

How foolish and naïve I was
I know I'll never reach perfection
But thank God for His love and grace
That points me in the right direction.

We must always be on guard
For Satan's demons are sly
They can infiltrate our souls
Quicker than the blink of an eye.

By what name are these demons known?
Murder, lust, idolatry, pride
Hatred, anger, jealousy, selfishness
Will lead to Christian suicide.

If they make the slightest inroad
Then, they can gain further ground
And for us, it gets easier
Once we let our defenses down.

So when I awake each morning
I relinquish to God the day
Only leaning on God's strength, not mine
Can I banish Satan's demons away.

The Day of Judgment

God's Judgment Day is coming
We know not where nor when
In the twinkling of an eye
Christ will come again.

We envision a God of love
But He is also a God of wrath
And the God that we encounter
Is determined by our chosen path.

Those who worshiped idols
Shall fear the wrath to come
Though prophets issued warnings
To sin they did succumb.

Wheat will be parted from the chaff
Goats divided from the lambs,
And those who sought not the Lord
Will bear Satan's pentagrams.

So hold fast to this revelation
Which for centuries has been proclaimed
Remember, Christ died upon a cross
If asked, "Why?" He'd speak your name.

Please do not ignore Christ
He longs to claim your soul
Before the Day of Judgment
Place your name on heaven's roll.

A Mission Encounter

I went to feed the hungry
And volunteered my time
While their needs were met
God spiritually met mine.

Each hungry face held a story
Of broken dreams in the past
Mirroring struggles and defeat
Worldly things vanish so fast.

There are many kinds of hunger
We see throughout our life
Some are inferior, others noble
But only Christ can ease our strife.

We all come to that time of reckoning
When we know, we're not in control
And realize, we must make a choice
As to whom we release our soul.

Christ is the only answer
He, our precious Savior, we claim
Though not the easy way
 He never changes; He stays the same.

In view of the choice we've made
We need to share what we know
And feed the hungry who pass our way
So to Christ's Banquet, together, we go.

Show Me

We live in a 'show me' world
Which wants proof and needs to see
When we say we are Christians
Our actions bear out that decree.

Our lives are under a microscope
People listen when we talk
But our most important witness
Is if we successfully 'walk the walk'.

What's visible in our daily lives
Not just Sunday while at church
Self-righteousness, gossip, jealousy
So diligent is the world's search.

For if one of God's chosen fails
Satan will dance with glee
Saying you, too, are of the world
And are really no better than me.

We are by no means perfect
God's not finished with us yet
We remain a work in progress
And still by temptations are beset.

Thankfully, we are a branch of his vine
Striving for the spirit's fruit to bear
Faithfulness, joy, patience and love
Share these with the world if you dare.

Rejoice when unsaved become believers
As God's kingdom on earth they have seen
And accepted His redemptive forgiveness
Gifts to all from the Nazarene.

My Role

Surely I was placed on earth
At this specific time and place
So I could accomplish some task
Not exist to just occupy space.

Time for me now seems to be
Quickly sliding out of control
Days and months spin faster
While I still seek my role.

The time that lies before me
Is much less than that gone by
What do I have to show for it
Am I just a mere passerby?

Will there be some evidence
Of my presence on this earth?
Will some of my accomplishments
Produce anything of worth?

Right now I stop to contemplate
Review, then forge ahead
If I've done good, repeat it
If not, consider this my watershed.

Yes, our days on earth are numbered
So we need to use them well
To make the world a better place
A Heaven on Earth in which to dwell.

May we complete our assigned tasks
With utmost joy, may I do mine
And in the years that remain for me
To the Lord's plan my life align.

Front Row Disciples

Reflect on the lives of disciples
And their commitment to be true
It seems simple on the surface
But, in truth, difficult to do.

The first disciples lived with Christ
Awed by His miracles firsthand
Witnessed Jesus heal the sick
The oppressed freed at His command.

Disciples were amazed by His teachings
They were touched, as was the crowd
Then ably assisted Christ in His work
As with His power they were endowed.

So what are true disciples' traits
What makes Christ love them so?
They're willing to be taught and led
Wherever He would have them go.

Disciples are eager to serve
But give God all the glory
Receptive to whatever miracles come
Gladly sharing the Good News story.

But front row seats have their price
Of things we hold most dear
Pride, control, and self-sufficiency
Perhaps, rejection the greatest fear.

Front row seat disciples
Rely on Christ's strength and direction
They applaud God's grace and mercy
Which led to their divine selection.

God's Super Bowl

If Christ were a Gator, 'Nole or Buc
Would we cheer Him aloud,
Follow every move He makes
Part of the enthusiastic crowd?

Proudly waving team colors
Attending each and every game
Ignoring the sacks and fumbles
Loyal, supportive, would we remain?

Lifting up our earnest prayers
That coaches make the right call
Thus bringing the taste of victory
And elation to one and all.

Christ is on the Lord's squad
Recruitment is still quite a task
No one cheers or attends each week
Carry His banner…don't even ask.

People might think we're fanatics
So we quietly mumble Amen
Always out for Number One
Team Spirit is void and broken.

Yes, the calls are ours to make
So why not convert our energy
Then reassess all of life's goals
And approach the game confidently.

We can't lose with God on the sidelines
He is the best coach that ever could be
So follow God's game plan
Then our team can claim victory!

DEVOTION

*For day after day they seek me out;
they seem eager to know my ways,
as if they were a nation that does
what is right…*

Isaiah 58:2

A Second Wedding

You wandered through life searching
For that special guy to marry
A soul mate to love and honor
But what you found was temporary.

Undaunted you renewed your search
Still hoping true love you would find
Then a special someone appeared
He was just what you had in mind.

So on your happy wedding day
You pledged your love and said, "I do"
And started your life as man and wife
With a wish of much happiness for you.

Our Bridegroom

Jesus Christ is the bridegroom
And we, the church, are His bride
He will protect and guide us
All we need He doth provide.

Marriage requires commitment
Devoted soul mates Christ needs
Those who gladly exalt Him
And follow wherever He leads.

This Groom is our Master
Who created all we survey
And because He greatly loves us
He, himself, our debts did pay.

Life will take on new meaning
This union we won't regret
All His promises Christ will keep
And our vows He will never forget.

The Race

A champion must be committed
Not haphazard, nor half-hearted
Straight is the gate; narrow the way
Read God's rules first; then get started.

The choice of teams only you can make
The way of the world or Christ
Your score will be totaled at the end
But won't balance out His sacrifice.

The race God sets before us
Is the battle for lost souls
We press towards the finish line
To win the prize, is our highest goal.

The rule book is the Holy Bible
The book of life contains your score
The goal is Eternal Salvation
The prize...life forever more.

Our Devotion

We worship God when times are good
When they are bad we ask, "Why me?"
We all face testing our faith
As did even the man of Galilee.

To what degree do we trust Him
This loving and mighty King?
Though we see Him not, He is near
For He's the Master of everything.

If we stop and examine our lives
Stepping out from behind our façade
Reach out to Him in childlike faith
We'll feel the presence of the Living God.

Pray constantly; take time to listen
Forget your way and rely only on His
If we remain loyal and obedient
He will lift us above our abyss.

God wants only the best for us
And if we give Him complete control
We can live a life abundantly blessed
And like the psalmist says
"It is well with my soul."

The Star of the Show

The things we do for honor and praise
Will someday be burned into ashes
For we will have received our reward
By shallow applause from the masses.

Only the things that have been done
In His name and for His glory
Will last and remain forever
And be part of heaven's story.

For when we magnify Christ's name
And exalt Him in all we do
While totally forgetting ourselves
Only then can His spirit shine through.

We are powerless without Him
Christ is the star of the show
And only by sharing what He's done
Can others His redemptive love know.

Nothing we've done or could ever do
Would in heaven assure us a place
So humbly praise the Master to all
As we witness, bathed in His grace.

Marriage Is God's Masterpiece

Today you begin your life together
By the joining of each heart
Two have now become one
You're blessed with a new start.

All the past trials are erased
Wisdom gleaned from them remains
And will help you as man and wife
To live and love as God ordains.

Of course there will be ups and downs
You're individuals… not the same
But if you adapt and compromise
Even brighter will burn love's flame.

And as each year comes and goes
Your happiness will increase
For love gives meaning to all things
Marriage is God's Masterpiece.

Lived right, it's God's finest blessing
So consider each other a treasure
Cherish, honor, trust and support
And enjoy a lifetime of pleasure.

Empathy

It seems as I've gotten older
My tear ducts have dried up
No longer gushing freely
If sweet or bitter my cup.

My cheeks would always dampen
At weddings, deaths or a birth
Denoting happiness or sadness
Even uncontrolled mirth.

Have I become hard-hearted
By feelings touched no longer
Withdrawn from cares of the world
Or have I just grown stronger?

Now my empathy shows itself
By a way of actively caring
I'll cry with you or do a task
Run errands or meal preparing.

These days my tears flow inside
As I try to meet your needs
And while you see no outside tears
Rest assured, my heart bleeds.

Friendship

To have a friend you must be one
A simple exercise in love
Showing concern and compassion
As decreed by our Father above.

For Christ gave us the Golden Rule
As an example of how we should live
And if someone asks a favor
Not one but two we should give.

Forgetting 'self' and thinking of others
Brings satisfaction beyond compare
No longer dwelling on our needs
Take this higher road if you dare.

You will reap abundant blessings
As you fellowship with each other
For God, in His wisdom knew
Our need for peace with our brother.

Our happiness is far greater
When with a friend we share
Our burdens become much lighter
When confronted by a pair.

So if a full rich life you want
Reach out and make a friend
You'll both be happy with a relationship
And by the many blessings God will send.

Servile Master

Daydreaming, half awake
Back in time I was transported
To the disciples' Last Supper
And to Christ I exhorted…

You wish to wash my feet, Lord
I cannot allow this task
It is the job of a servant
Why do you even ask?

Son of God, King of Kings
Why should you kneel by me?
You granted mercy and forgiveness
From sin you set my soul free.

You gazed upon my darkest deed
And through your redemptive act
You purified your wayward lamb
Making love and compassion a fact.

Abba, Father provide my needs
Protect your trusting child
Keep me cleansed from head to feet
Till I, like you, become servile.

For not by talents, nor by strength
Can we claim our salvation
Only through our faith and trust
In the Maker of all Creation.

His Name

Christ's name is above all names
Jehovah, the Prince of Peace.
He who created the universe
Can command stormy seas to cease.

How mighty is the great I AM
Who gives our existence meaning.
And sacrificed His only Son
In payment for our redeeming.

Lion of Judah by some He's called
Rose of Sharon, Light of the World.
Forever bathed in righteousness
Against sin His banner is unfurled.

At His name every knee shall bow
As we give Him our honor and praise.
The Everlasting Father we laud
When our thanks and prayers we raise.

The Mighty Counselor will guide us
Pointing out the path we should trod.
He will send the Holy Spirit
To lead us ever closer to God.

There are many names but just one Lord
Who is worthy of our ardent esteem.
He will answer to whatever name is called,
But forever His name is SUPREME.

Transcending Love

How can love be measured
By what standard might we gauge?
If a description were penned
A thousand words would fill a page.

There are many kinds of love
Parent-child, husband-wife,
Love of knowledge, food, music
Dear friends met throughout life.

Some loves are tender-caring
Others selfish, cold, unkind.
Many choose a gentle soul
But some to love are blind.

The love that transcends all
Is that which is heaven sent,
Given by Christ, God's own Son
To negate our devilment.

Christ's love nailed Him to a cross
Where He willingly took our place,
Proving His deep love for us
And also, the whole human race.

Only His love can blot out all sin
Then unbind and set us free,
With this love we are born again
And can claim Christ's pedigree.

A Christlike life is all God asks
Whereby we love and then we share,
To make the world His Valentine
As His kingdom on earth we declare.

FORGIVENESS

*You are kind and forgiving, O Lord;
Abounding in love to all who call to you.*

Psalm 86:5

Christ's Invitation

Christ issues His great invitation
To every woman and man
Who thirst for the water He giveth
So the dryness of sin He can ban.

Christ forgives our many sins
By granting us a reprieve
We're then set on the path of truth
Our journey with Him we cleave.

We're no longer aloof…in exile
But delivered into Christ's fold
Thereby, blessed with joy and peace
For we are finally made whole.

Across time Christ's invitation stands
"Come, drink and thirst no more."
All who accept this plea, in faith
With love He will transform and restore.

My Life's Story

I searched life's meaning
In a world fickle and vain.
Betrayed, discouraged, broken
I retreated in sorrow and pain.

I felt alone and abandoned
By all whom I'd held dear.
Darkness wrapped its veil about me
My breath quickened as did my fear.

Deep within my cry broke forth
"Lord, I've no one to turn to but you."
Then so gently He took my hand
And said, "I'll make everything new."

God scooped up a handful of mercy
From the deep basin of His grace.
My sins were washed away
Each stain gone… without a trace.

Since I made that ardent decision
I now praise Him with honor and glory.
Our merciful God who heard my cry
With love, rewrote my life's story.

Christ's Banquet

Will you be invited to feast
At the banquet of Christ, our Lord
One of the blessed partakers
One of the Father's adored?

Or will you sup with Judas
With betrayal the main entree
Dining only on wormwood and gall
When from the Lord you did stray?

God's children will sit at His table
While the lost stand outside and gaze
By their body language and stance
All can sense their abject malaise.

By acknowledging Christ as Savior
They, too, could receive His grace
With that single admission
At Christ's table they'd have a place.

Their hunger forever was sated
They'd join the rejoicing throng
In fellowship with the Trinity
Forever singing Eternity's song.

With Nothing

There's an oft quoted adage
Its truth many believe,
'With nothing you came into the world
And with nothing you will leave.'

I don't agree with that statement
If I left today, I'm not as I came,
For since I accepted Christ as Savior
My life hasn't been the same.

Having worldly goods I had nothing
Life had no meaning; empty I felt,
My future seemed bleak and frightening
Until finally on my knees, I knelt.

Since the day I made my decision
The world is a much different place,
I'm no longer the sinner I was
For I've looked on the Savior's face.

So the nothing I brought into the world
Has become a glorious thing,
I have joy, salvation, eternal life
All gifts to me from the King.

Set Your Course

There are times I've prayed and felt
It didn't go above my ceiling
Not even an inch heavenward
In truth, that's a scary feeling.

I asked, "Are you listening, Lord?"
Ironically, then I realized
I'm the one who did not hear
When to me Christ verbalized.

I know I am self-centered
Trying to solve needs on my own
Not turning problems over to Him
Perhaps, in my voice, a carnal tone.

I didn't mean to get in Christ's way
In Philippians, Paul sets the course
Above all, Paul's choice is Jesus
And for us there is no other source.

All things work together for good
In Jesus I have all I need
Not my will but His be done
May the Scriptures we always heed.

Forgiveness

If Jesus forgave like we do
Our future would be very dim
For if we withhold forgiveness
We should expect the same from Him.

We cling to yesterday's hurtful slights
Reliving each trite and petty thing
Yet we expect our slate wiped clean
Thinking we can fool the King of Kings.

He understands our heart's intent
And delves deep into our mind
Seeking evidence of lessons learned
Likewise, "Do unto others, be kind."

We're measured by His 'Golden Rule'
Will He determine we are lacking?
For if we're meted what we deserve
Christ would surely send us packing.

However, He loves us so much
So sinless on a cross, Christ died
Our transgressions would be forgiven
And we could be His worthy bride.

So release all that would hinder you
From claiming Jesus Christ as Lord
Forgive others as you were forgiven
And become one of the Savior's adored.

DEPENDENCE

*"I am the vine; you are the branches.
If a man remains in me and I in him,
he will bear much fruit; apart from
me you can do nothing."*

John 15:5

Your Choice

When they've erred, some jokingly say
"The devil made me do it."
God gave us the freedom of choice
In truth, they're the ones who blew it.

Some folks can't admit their wrongs
Because of their ego and self pride
But Jesus Christ who was sinless
Was nailed to a cross and died.

Satan's plan: that we would do his bidding
For he delights in bringing us down
While God offers us love, mercy and grace
And assures us a heavenly crown.

Your choice

The Battle

When Jesus washed away my sin
I was filled with enormous relief
I thought finally the battle was over
My, how naïve was that belief.

For Satan increases his efforts
When to Christ we're reconciled
He never quits or admits defeat
When we remain Jesus' child.

Each day brings another skirmish
Attacked from without and within
But armed with Christ's strength
Each evil battle we will win.

This war against the devil continues
And will till the last trumpets sound
Announcing Christ's return to earth
Revealing God's truth so profound.

Control Released

Oft times I run on empty
Exhausted – out of gas
Burned out and drained by stress
Praying, "Please, world, me bypass."

Going round and round in circles
Everything beyond my control
Defeated and mired in self-pity
Instead of being a witness so bold.

Questioning unanswered prayer
When doubt dwells in faith's place
God surely is so dismayed
At how I'm running my race.

God reveals this comforting fact
He loves me and has promised to provide
Strength for my tribulations and trials
Since I've claimed Him as my Guide.

I've now released control to Christ
Who wills that we study and learn
The truths that only God can impart
Now refreshed, refilled, hope returns.

List Your Blessings

When you become discouraged
Stuck in a mood that's blue
Make a list of the blessings
God has bestowed on you.

We take these blessings for granted
And consider them our due
Treating God as our servant
When actually the reverse is true.

Are pride and self-importance
A part of our daily lives
Do we dismiss our faults or failures,
Allow arrogance to survive?

Christ expects us to be humble
This sinful world to serve
Giving Christlike compassion
So His love, the lost might observe.

Christ issues a challenge
To the world the Gospel proclaim
Thus, bringing forth fruit for eternity
Which is the reason God's Son came.

The Storms of Life

"Fear not for I am with you,"
The Lord whispers again and again.
Still we claim not His promises
Losing all we might attain.

We think that we can sail our ship
Through the treacherous waters of life
Knowing not what dangers await
The disappointments and the strife.

Then in a twinkling of an eye
Comes a storm we can't control.
Our ship is torn asunder
And the struggle takes its toll.

Frightened, weary, again we hear
His whisper, voiced with tenderness,
"Be not afraid; I am with you, and
 Will guide you through your distress."

So venture out, not on your own
For a fool the world will devour
Instead, remain protected and safe
In the promise of the Lord's mighty power.

Who Moved?

Have you felt so close to God
Then seemed to move away
Not a sudden separation
But an erosion day by day?

Did you stop studying scripture
Spend less time on your knees in prayer
Not claiming Christ as your source
No longer wanting to be His heir?

The measure between indifference and faith
Is the distance between heaven and hell
And your faithfulness is a necessity
If in heaven you wish to dwell.

We can't take Christ's love for granted
It must be acknowledged every day
For through His Word, worship and prayer
He will lift us above the world's fray.

So beware of temptations that dazzle
Don't let the world entice you
Remember the supreme sacrifices made
And to Jesus, remain ever true.

Jesus Has Been There

Have you ever been betrayed
Or faced the sting of rejection
Felt abandoned…all alone
Met with undeserved objection?

Jesus suffered all these things
And knows what you're going through
He was born to die on a cross
For lowly sinners like me and you.

Despite all the Master faced
He endured right to the end
Fulfilling prophesy that in three days
From whence He came, He'd return again.

He neither rejects nor betrays us
But surrounds us with His grace
Our souls are filled with utmost joy
For us, He's prepared a place.

He trod the road before us
Paying all our tolls on the way
So we, too, might become conquerors
And on Heaven's highway always stay.

He Waits

Christ patiently waits outside the door
Hoping we will ask Him to come in
Unaware of His boundless love for us
Sadly, we remain mired down in sin.

He knows that we are not perfect
But with grace He will take us 'as is'
He died for us on Calvary's cross
Made that sacrifice so we could be His.

And when we decide to wander
He patiently watches for our return
We... the inherent Prodigal Son
Cause Christ distress and concern.

Why did God choose you or even me?
What do we have that the Savior needs?
This simple fact... He made and loves us
In spite of failures and shameful deeds.

Never forcing if He's not invited
The choice is entirely ours
When conviction moves us to His side
His divine faith our doubt devours.

God won't turn His back on us
Or let us face our trials alone
He has been there and knows the danger
And has conquered the 'great unknown'.

Road of Life

How strange is the journey of life
Looking back in retrospect
What we strive and wish for
Is not what we always get.

The rain soaks the just and unjust
Sometimes we're caught in a shower
And can't seem to conquer that storm
Without God's mighty power.

We know not what waits before us
The future is in Christ's hands
We must travel one day at a time
And, in faith, follow His commands.

Christ is the one true signpost
That gives us proper direction
And only if we follow His path
Will we receive His divine protection.

When we grow weak and weary
Us, in His arms, He will carry
There we'll be sheltered and safe
With Jesus Christ…our sanctuary.

What better route could we choose
Than that of Christ, our King
His way is the only road
Toward life's joy in everything.

Last Days

Christ's return is coming
At any moment it could be
The signs are all about us
Read again the prophesies.

Israel's rebirth has occurred
Morality is at new lows
Famines, wars and violence
All seeds that Satan sows.

Disasters are rampant about us
The antichrist will deceive
Nations will foolishly worship him
His blasphemies they'll believe.

The mark of the beast is theirs
Facing God's fury and wrath
But the saints' names are written
In the Book of Life God hath.

Christ will judge the living and dead
Everything will be made brand new
No more death, fear, worry or pain
And finally the devil will get his due.

What day or time will Jesus come?
God and Son knows when and where
So remain ever ready, alert, on guard
Till we see Christ's arrival in the air.

The Good Shepherd

Jesus is the Good Shepherd
Who laid down His life for His sheep
Though most powerful, He's also tender
For Christ bestows love abundantly deep.

He was once an innocent lamb
Sinless, He was given in sacrifice
Whereby Christ became our blessed savior
Who bought us, gladly paying our price.

He's promised to care for His flock
And knows each of us by name
He senses even our darkest thoughts
But still to share His love He came.

The Good Shepherd knows each crevice
Each rock which might cause us to fall
He will gently guide us to safety
If we will answer to His call.

Do we poor lambs recognize His voice?
"I am the truth, the light, the way."
Eternal life with Our Shepherd
Will be ours, if by His side, we'll stay.

What glory is ours if we follow
To whatever paths He may lead
Our faith and trust will increase
If His Holy Spirit we heed.

What If, Lord?

What if I'd never met you, Lord
Walking through life continually bored
Slipping backward instead of forward
Instead of rejoicing in you?

What if I'd never seen your light
Feeling the pain of the world's cruel bite
Joining the battle but losing the fight
Instead of claiming your strength?

What if I'd closed my eyes to your call
Never to feast in your banquet hall
On my menu only wormwood and gall
Instead of becoming your child?

What if I'd never been born again
All my sins on me would remain
Never to share your heavenly domain
Instead of receiving your grace?

I fall down before you, Savior divine
I am yours, hallelujah, you are mine
A fruit-bearing branch of the Master's vine
   I REJOICE
   I AM STRONG
  I AM YOUR CHILD
   I RECEIVE
  I AM MADE WHOLE

LISTENING

*My dear brothers, take note of this:
Everyone should be quick to listen,
slow to speak and slow to become angry…*

James 1: 19

Whisper His Name

What problems are you facing
Knowing not which way to turn
Feeling alone and helpless
For hope and peace you yearn.

The world can be uncaring
Ignoring many needs
So turn to the One who loves you
His heart for you did bleed.

Christ is waiting to help you
To share His strength and power
If you will just whisper His Name
You will feel His presence every hour.

Why Me?

When faced with problems or trials
Many people ask God, "Why me?"
They feel they live a saintly life
And don't deserve such misery.

There are a lot of sinful folks, Lord
Who live by their rules, not yours
Enjoying the world's material things
Although I'm not keeping score.

O.K., Lord, I'm not the one to judge
I know I'll never reach perfection
Instead of counting another's faults
My own could stand correction.

So help me work on my flaws
And grant me more humility
So I might emulate you, master
And retain my Eternal guarantee.

Worry Not

Life today is so stressful
Each day adds to the mix
We go from problem to problem
Hoping we will find a quick fix.

We plod on through each distress
Losses occur, friendships fade
Many issues need to be faced
As we often rue the choices made.

In this hectic world we admit
God is sometimes thrust aside
We are undermined by fear
Which derails our spiritual ride.

Christ said, "Worry not for tomorrow"
Help for our burdens He will give
Endure each day as it comes
Honoring Him by the way we live.

Our Future

Some folks are so organized
Their whole future is planned out
And want no sudden surprises
They're in complete control, no doubt.

God laughs when He gets their message
For He's the Master Creator, no less
And doesn't need help from mortals
Whose talent lies in making a mess.

I can't predict what today will bring
Much less years and years ahead
I'm well aware of my limitations
So I'll depend on the Lord instead.

With free choice, we can thwart God's plan
Like the fools who think they know best
But God will guide us through good and bad
When Christ, our Savior, we have professed.

Self Inventory

Stop and take inventory of your life
Kind things done; times selfishness won
Weighing the good against bad
What's been done in the name of the Son.

Goodness will last forever
Into ashes, the rest will burn
Many of our peers we may fool
But Christ our hearts can discern.

He looks not at our appearances
But sees right to our core
Past our pious 'holier than thou'
When we ignore the plight of the poor.

We quote Scripture as we witness
But our lives speak louder still
Minuses cancel out the pluses
Regardless, Christ loves us still.

Undeserving, He gives us grace
His agape love voids all our sin
If we but reconnect with Christ
And our hearts ask Him back in.

Shared Whispers

When Christ whispers in my ear
I record the words I'm told
But hesitated to share them
Till He said, "Step out; be bold."

So if you read my poetry
Please be constantly aware
It's not pointing to you, friend
But to me, Christ's arrogant heir.

For I am flawed like many
Facing daily temptations and trials
Only Christ can impart this grace
And save me from Satan's wiles.

Find the love between the lines
Christ understands us all so well
And intercedes on our behalf
So we won't feel the flames of Hell.

I shall remain mindful of Christ
To His thoughts strive to stay true
Hoping you will feel His presence
And devotion to Him ensue.

Our Shepherd

Like sheep, we are selfish and stubborn
As we blindly tread the path to hell.
Our spirits are shriveled and impotent
As we merrily ride Satan's carousel.

If we listen to the world's voice
From righteousness we will stray.
But Christ can free us from our sins
To fresh pastures, He'll show the way.

Our Shepherd calls out to us in love
As fretful sheep, do we hear His voice?
He wants to protect and care for us
Hear or ignore His word – our choice.

The Shepherd wants to walk with us
And He gave His life for us all.
With Christ, we can live abundantly
If we will hear and answer His call.

Through His teachings, we're aware
He desires that all lost sheep be found.
He asks that we, too, search and witness
Leading them to paths, homebound.

What great rejoicing in Jesus' flock
When sheep are found, no longer lost.
For this purpose our Shepherd came
And for our sins, lovingly paid our cost.

Night of Wonder

I donned my gown and turned off the light
Slid 'neath the covers to welcome sleep.
Instead I thought of the day I'd had
And I uncontrollably began to weep.

Why must life be so hard and unfair
Out of control, everyone so wrong?
What can I do in my circumstances
To be more confident and strong?

I heard a voice saying, "Come unto me."
I turned to see who was speaking,
"I am your Father; you are my child,
The lost I am always seeking."

I wasn't lost; I knew right where I was,
I shook as I asked, "Who's there?"
Christ spoke, "Fear not; calm your soul,
 For all your troubles and trials I'll bear."

Bolder, I queried, "Do I know you?"
He replied, "Not as well as you should.
I'm Jesus, I died to save you
At Calvary, upon a cross of wood."

He told me then of His love and grace
His sacrifice which erased my sin.
In prayer I asked His forgiveness
And instantly salvation I did win.

How drastically my life has changed
I'm now His child, no longer alone.
Since that night He claimed me
And made His presence known.

Who Knew?

WHO KNEW...
That sweet Babe upon the hay
With an angelic face
Was sent here on a mission
To save the human race?

WHO KNEW...
God loved us so much
He'd send His only son
To die on the cross for us
Though His sins were none?

WHO KNEW...
The twelve disciples He chose
Would share His Gospel of love
Telling all the world that Christ
Was the Savior sent from above?

WHO KNEW...
The number of His believers
In church there would be
Still, after two thousand years
Crowds are saved and set free?

WHO KNEW...
We'd be part of God's family
From Hell to Heaven our view
Unworthy His grace and mercy
Christ made us all brand new?

WHO KNEW...
The Father, Son and
Holy Spirit...of course.

Thoughts Shared

When my mind is clear
And my soul is calm
God whispers in my ear.
And what He says
I share with you
And pray you may hear
The truth within
The words I write,
And you can understand.
For each of us
He has a mission
This is mine per His command.

It seems a channel
I have become
I know not how nor why.
I'm not learned
Nor profound.
No special person, I.
Still the phrases
Come tumbling out
As I ponder their content.
Then at last
I grasp some truth
And understand our Lord's intent.

In conclusion
God wants me
To take these words to heart.
Stay the path
He's set for me
With the Bible as my chart.
Though these thoughts
Address my needs
You, too, may feel their prod.
If so, join with me
To journey into
A deeper relationship with God.

Time For New Wine

When Jesus left the carpenter shop
He knew that it was time
To become the awaited Messiah
And to that cross, start His climb.

It was time to begin preaching
God's message, and heal the sick too
Christ knew exactly what lay in store
But willingly, died for me and you.

His love and devotion paid the price
Our past pardoned, our future secure
No other would be so forgiving
To those, whose lives were impure.

From His Holy basin, Christ scooped up
Enough mercy to wash away our sins
Removing us from Satan's darkness
Pouring new wine in our old wineskins.

Now we know it's time again
To witness what Christ has done
Not just for us, but all mankind
For there are still many to be won.

We must be about our Father's business
"Time waits for no one," it's been said,
It's time to put our hand to the plow
While rejoicing what waits ahead.

And when our time is finally gone
We're hopeful that we will hear,
"Well done, good faithful servant,
Welcome, your loved ones are near."

MEMORIES

*Remember the days of old;
consider the generations long past.*

Deuteronomy 32: 7a

Fighting for Freedom

America called; you answered
Leaving love ones and comforts behind
Joining with others for this cause
To fight terror and save humankind.

Sent to the Mideast so far away
Risk and danger at every hand
To conquer Al Qaida and the terrorists
And rescue Iraq and Afghanistan.

To you and brave ones everywhere
Who lay their lives down on the line
Proudly defending freedom for all
You are keeping 'Old Glory' enshrined.

There is a God and He cares for you
He knows your name and what you need
And with the many prayers on your behalf
Your mission will surely succeed.

For three years I shared this poem with military men and women along with a handwritten letter.

Broken Vessels

How difficult to see your loved one
Losing his memory day by day
Erasing part of your married life
How heavy your heart must weigh.

Your conversations now are limited
As Jerry's understanding comes and goes
This man, once so intelligent,
More like a young child daily grows.

This burden so heavy and hard to bear
You do with deep devotion and love
Honoring your vows 'for better or worse'
Receiving strength from the Lord above.

We wish we could relieve your stress
And would gladly help with any task
You have our prayers… if anything else
Please, friend, don't hesitate to ask.

There's no way I can understand
What you're going through
But I hope this poem will tell you
How much I sympathize with you.

My Father

My father left when I was two
He was never here to guide me
To be an example of the man
I'd choose to stand beside me.

I first encountered Christ as a teen
He asked that I be reconciled
Recalling hurts from my earthly dad
I quickly cried, "I'm not your child."

Grieved, He spoke of His death on the cross
Which gave humanity choice for a new start
I sensed Christ's love and felt His peace
And then slowly surrendered my heart.

Doubtful at first, I learned to trust
This Father like none I had known
Who promised He'd never forsake me
And eagerly sought me to be His own.

He gave me value and self esteem
Values lacking when I was young
And I'm no longer a 'fatherless child'
Since to my Heavenly Father I've clung.

Our Daughter

Alone, you needed someone to care
In the blink of an eye, Dad and I were there
So excited about the life we'd share.
      Suzanne Kay Jones

You wanted us; we wanted you
So God decided the thing to do
Was to form a family all brand new.
      Suzanne Kay Jones

Our grateful hearts opened wide
And made a place for you inside
Our future dreams to you are tied.
      Suzanne Kay Jones

Our pride is there for all to see
Now, forever our daughter you'll be
A new branch of the Jones family tree.
      Suzanne Kay Jones

As happy parents we now profess
Our prayers for you that God will bless
Your life with utmost joy and happiness.
      Suzanne Kay Jones

Our Sixtieth Anniversary

The precious diamond of our love
Has shone brightly for sixty years
Angels have watched over us
As we shared happiness and tears.

Faithfully we kept our vows
To always love, trust and obey
Daily living the best we could be
Touching many lives along the way.

How happy our lives together
Among family and many friends
And today with them we celebrate
Toasting a love that never ends.

May God continue to bless us
As we recall days of the past
And may each added year we share
Be more blessed than the last.

Goodbye, My Love

Jimmy was an extraordinary guy
Kind and caring…the love of my life.
He proposed to me sixty years ago
And I very happily became his wife.

The many plans that we had made
Disappeared at last Saturday's dawn.
And today, I am a sad, lonely widow
Because my loving husband is gone.

The vows spoken at our wedding
'For Better or Worse' was the verse.
The Better lasted sixty wonderful years
Now, all alone, I face the Worse.

He has joined parents, family, son Neil
God planned a great celebration
To welcome this good faithful servant
Who earned his heavenly graduation.

We each have our Jimmy memories
We'd have missed much had we not met,
In his special way, he touched us all
JAMES W. JONES, we will never forget!

Two Minus One

Life has become so lonely
Since I lost the man I love
The one I shared my life with
Is now watching from above.

I can no longer turn to him
As I struggle through the days
With no one to wash and cook for
It's like walking through a maze.

I remember many things we shared
He was most considerate and kind
This man I loved so deeply
Is still with me in my mind.

This house is now so empty
And forever changed is my life
Today I am his lonely widow
Yesterday… Jimmy's happy wife.

I thank God for blessings
My family and caring friends
The love, concern and prayers
Who, on my behalf, daily sends.

So, with your help, Lord I'll hang on
Here, on earth, I'll keep marking time
Until that day that I will rejoin
That wonderful husband of mine.

The Columbia Tragedy

Sixteen minutes before landing
The Columbia's fiery crash
Took the life of seven astronauts
Leaving behind only rubble and ash.

In the blue skies over Texas
This stark tragedy took place
The earth, scorched and charred
Ended this experiment in space.

We all looked on with horror
As the media replayed the tape
Again we saw the disintegration
With teary eyes, our mouths agape.

Technology designed this craft
So throughout space it could soar
Unlocking universal secrets
Another dimension to explore.

But frailty is found in all of life
With disappointment its nearest kin
And though the seven now are gone
Others will rise where they've been.

We know lives have been sacrificed
So we might learn space's mysteries
But know also God is in control
While we are only earth's trustees.

For He who created everything
Knows all before it is asked
One day we will view space firsthand
As Heaven's threshold we've passed.

HUMOR

*…but the Lord laughs at the wicked,
for he knows their day is coming.*

Psalm 37:13

Birthday Nightmare

Mirror, mirror
Now I see
Over the years
What happened to me
But a tuck here
And a stitch there
Will bring an end
To my…
Birthday Nightmare!

Good Morning

Sometimes I'm not in the mood
A cheery "Good Morning" to hear
Until I've been awake for an hour
They can leap off the nearest pier.

Morning isn't the time for clear thought
That's why God created the afternoon
A time when 'night owls' are alert
Then our thinking we can fine tune.

Otherwise, my flag is at half-mast
I'm just naught flying in the breeze
And in the Monopoly game of life
I'll take my turn later, please.

Too Much Stuff

Have you noticed the storage barns
That are popping up everywhere
All because we have too much stuff
Our homes have no space to spare.

We look through catalogues and ads
And covet each new fad and style
What we need… we must have it
But then tire of it in a little while.

Foolishly we convince ourselves
To pay a storage monthly fee
Instead of sharing our surplus
With some worthwhile charity.

Many folks would be appreciative
To receive some things they need
And we'd have the satisfaction
That comes from doing a good deed.

My Epitaph

Don't take life so seriously
Be thankful you're still alive
Live each day to the fullest
Before you take your final dive.

Some might say, "How morbid"
But I just chuckle and laugh
If they knew, they'd think me bizarre
'Cause I've written my own epitaph.

Why should some bloke have that task?
I know my own self better than many
Besides, they might share all my faults
I'd rather all thought I didn't have any.

Who'd argue with a voice from the grave
Fearing they might evoke some curse?
And if my eulogy isn't finished yet
Listen as you walk past the hearse.

The Aging Game

When people reach their mature years
Their talk centers on doctors and ills
And it seems a contest develops
Who is 'King and Queen of the Pills'?

Today our social life consists
Of doctor visits and lab tests
Open your mouth; bend over, please!
But we're still here, and are blessed.

We often share old memories
Comparing today with long ago
It's difficult to remember names and places
Our speedometers seem stuck on SLOW.

This poem wasn't meant to be morbid
We still have a lot 'on the ball'
So throw it, bounce it, while you can
Until you get that heavenly call!

Forever Young

Eyesight's gone
Hearing's poor
Memory's flown
Out the door.

Body parts droop
Heading due south
Not many teeth
Left in my mouth.

Skin has sagged
If snipped loose
Another person
It would produce.

So many things
Now in the past
Even the sex flag
Flies at half-mast.

My boat has sailed
My spring has sprung
But in my mind
I'm forever young!

A High School Reunion

Those glorious days of black and gold
Didn't prepare us for growing old.
Our sleek trim bodies, full heads of hair
We cruised through life without a care.

But lately, when in the mirror we look
The image we see really leaves us shook.
The crow's feet and wrinkles on that stranger
Leaves my eternal youth in mortal danger.

As we return to this hallowed hall
We see reality has touched us all
Some look the same; others we haven't a clue
You don't remember me, and I don't know you.

We've come to celebrate 50 years gone by
To share our memories of old Plant High.
The aging Panthers are still able to growl
Not one of us is ready to 'throw in the towel'.

    So…
Happy 50th Reunion; we're glad you came,
Without you it wouldn't have been the same.

Calling All Worrywarts

Listen up all you worrywarts
I've planned an intervention
Take these words I share with you
With an ounce or two of prevention.

Things that you're hung up on
Very seldom ever come to pass
Your foot jammed on that pedal
Will burn up all your gas.

If something major should occur
You'll need that gas and more
So don't go looking for trouble
Till it's knocking at your door.

Finally, when you hear that knock
I'll tell you what you should do
Call up a compassionate friend
Troubles are lighter when shared by two.

With those 'what ifs' and 'maybes'
Your life needs some perspective
So do it…don't make me worry
That you will ignore my directive.

Mature Love

Love is always changing
It never stays the same
It begins with an attraction
That fans into a flame.

You finally meet that someone
Meant for you and you alone
One who will fill your future
With more happiness ever known.

As you and your mate mature
The word 'love' gets a new definition
No red hot flashes of hormones
Nor floor boarding of your ignition.

That's part of foolhardy youth
But mature love is not ho-hum
It has a more leisurely pace
As we march to a different drum.

Yes, red rockets glare no longer
But volumes still can be said
You're still in love with each other
Now looking forward to what's ahead.

What's Your Name?

A strange thing happened yesterday
Over the store's crowd I glanced
I thought I recognized a face
So to the other aisle I pranced.

"Fancy meeting you here," I said
We stopped and chatted for awhile
Grandkids, politics, world events
Then, hoping I didn't sound senile.

I said, " I'm sorry, I must confess
I don't remember your name."
"How soon do you have to know?" she asked.
Embarrassed, her face was aflame.

I smiled, "It happens to all of us."
We laughed and talked some more
And when I returned home I thought
Who was that lady in the store?

We all have dying brain cells
Which accounts for a lapse or two
I won't worry about instant recall
For neither can she identify you.

Insomnia

Like a runaway train
On a mountain steep
My wheels keep spinning
When I try to sleep.

If my brain had gears
I'd shift into PARK
For I need to rest
Enveloped by the dark.

But think I must
Of this and then that
Get up, lie down
Give my pillow a pat.

On my side, on my back
I turn and then twist
I started counting sheep
But several I missed.

Never mind, I've lost count
Which awakens me more
Now it's time to get up
And not once did I snore.

Ring-a-Dingy

Cell phones have introduced
A new way of being rude.
What gives a user license
To air their pompous attitude?

The world doesn't revolve around them
These hotshots must always be on tap.
They don't care who they might annoy
As they loudly continue to carp and yap.

They don't respect the rights of others
They talk, carelessly driving with one hand.
At meetings, movies, even in church
They haughtily ignore any reprimand.

Rude ringing doesn't denote status
Today, everyone has a cell phone too.
And if only I knew your number
I'd have a few choice words for you.

I don't want to hear your conversation
Who you're dating, your last big deal.
Just quietly hand over your weapon
So I can finally enjoy my meal.

Politics

Claws are bared and tongues wag
On today's political scene
The personal attacks on candidates
Are strident and downright mean.

The media promotes these brawls
For they lead to increased ratings
But the viciousness of the tirades
Voters find very aggravating.

Each candidate berates the others
And minimizes their credentials
To me, the dissenter, himself
Is devoid of any potential.

It surely was a politician who coined
The phrase, 'good guys finish last'
But I think, come election day
My vote for the good guy I'll cast.

At times amidst the election
If I believed all that was said
I wouldn't vote for a single candidate
For government doesn't need another
BLOCKHEAD!

Too Young To Be This Old

I hoped that time would stand still
So I'd never have to get old
I had endurance and good health
Couldn't wait for each day to unfold.

Then the years started rolling by
And quickly gathered NASCAR speed
"I'm too young to be this old," I cried
And that's become my rallying creed.

Who cares about senior discounts
They are meant for the very mature
I can still 'kick over the traces'
Proving to all I still can endure.

I feel an ache every now and then
And realize there are changes ahead
But when looking back at the past
By AARP, I was blindly misled.

I'm still active and involved
But now at a much slower pace
My birthday candles caught fire
But I'm still running life's race.

Vanity's Woes

What is that ugly glob
Hanging from my arms?
It seems to be human skin
Whatever it is
It's contagious
Now growing under my chin.

It repeats each
Jiggly movement
Dangling there for all to see
When brave enough
I peek in a mirror
That can't be part of me!

An occasional
Wrinkle I accept
For it lies there smug and staid
Not particularly
Embarrassing
But expected as 'my bloom' fades.

This unsightly mess
Really troubles me
I know cosmetics won't hide it
So then I decided to
'Throw in the towel'
 I'm sure that I can't fight it.

Patience Wins

We're all in such a hurry
Can't sit around and wait
We favor only instant things
 Take your time not on your slate.

Don't dream silly daydreams
No time to smell the roses
Don't just sit and waste your time
Or wander forty years like Moses.

Hop to it right this minute
I should have been here yesterday
This lane is moving far too slow
Finish first; then you can play.

Yes, patience is a virtue
A cousin to resignation
Granting bliss to those who wait
And are rewarded with jubilation.

If someone shoves or pushes you
Quickly step aside and state
"I'm just a tortoise-you're a hare,
What's your excuse for being late?"

I'm not for apathy or sloth
So don't misunderstand
'Good things do come to those who wait'
To quote the tortoise's game winning plan.

Eternal Youth

Those who seek eternal youth
Might think it's contained in a pill
Perhaps a new elixir or cream
Regardless how expensive the bill.

Who wouldn't like less wrinkles
Liposuction or a remolded 'bod'
But these different procedures
Attest our wish to improve on God.

We never truly seem satisfied
With just what we've been given
Inherited through family genes
To change ourselves we seem driven.

No one look is perfection
Stop searching for a cure-all
To achieve the changes you desire
Would take a major overhaul.

With who you are and how you look
Be comfortable in your own skin
For you're one of a kind…unique
So share the you that abides within.

You will then be a raving beauty
Not just another pretty face
The proof displayed for all to see
By your compassion, kindness and grace.

Not Ms. America

I notice my skin no longer fits
It sags to my elbows and knees
If shrinkage info is online
Quick, share it with me, please!

A turkey waddle 'neath my chin
Bags are present beneath each eye
When I squat down, I can't get up
Only a fullback has a bigger thigh.

My joints creak when I arise
Saddlebags cling to my hips
Hair grows in the strangest places
Moans and groans leave my lips.

My brain doesn't fare well either
It functions rather intermittently
If things don't improve real quick
I'll have to buy my own infirmary.

Many warnings I have heard
About getting 'over the hill'
I know I'm not Ms. America
But neither am I 'road kill'.

In view of all I've shared with you
I think I'm aging gracefully
My solution: break all mirrors.
That's how I cope with reality.

Over the Hill Blues

Another birthday has come and gone
But I truly don't feel passé or old
As long as I am still able to ignore
Those horrible age spots and a mole.

I hear a creak when I sit down
And give a groan when I arise
I feel a stiffness in all my joints
That double vision thing in my eyes.

To say nothing of my daily song
"Speak up louder… I can't hear a thing."
Foods I enjoyed I now can't eat
Metamusil, your praises I sing!

All sidewalks are built uphill now
I perspire and wheeze as I walk
And seem quickly to run out of gas
My memory is slow and delays my talk.

At times I notice my socks don't match
Other days I don two different shoes
I'll soon need a wig for my bald spots
I've got those 'Over the Hill Blues'.

Which means although I still feel young
A jokester said, "I've felt you; you do feel old."
But with silver in both my hair and teeth
Regardless of age, I'm finally worth
My weight in GOLD!

Senior Moments

As I age, I find instant recall
Becomes an elusive thing.
My brain goes on vacation
Not returning till next spring.

Don't ask what I had for lunch
That was at least an hour ago.
Pairing names with proper faces
Makes my recollective juices flow.

Of late, my pump has run dry
Due to a severe memory drought.
From my speech I've eliminated
The phrase…'without a doubt'.

When I try to recall an event
I'm met with an impregnable wall.
As the tide ebbs out on my brain waves
All I can do is stutter and stall.

So if I should pass you by one day
Without a nod, greeting or glance
Chalk it up to a 'senior moment'
And, please, give me another chance.

And, perhaps, on our next meeting
I'll say "Hello" and call out your name.
Should your response be a blank stare
I'll know 'senior moments' are to blame.

Her Silent Love

They often sit reading quietly
With nary a thought to share.
She stretched out on the sofa
He slumped in his easy chair.

For an hour not a word is said
He's gone to sleep, she notes.
He can't watch TV with his eyes closed
Her turn to be 'Queen of the remote'.

When she gets up to get a snack
Her guy finally opens his eyes.
"Bring me a glass of milk, please
And a couple of those Moon Pies."

Refreshed, he settles down again
She asks, "Would you like more?"
But the only reply she receives
Is a loud house-rattling snore.

Before you think, how boring
Some things you must understand.
When two have merged into one
Their love many years has spanned.

No need for words; a look will do
Along with a smile and a gentle touch.
They can finish each others' sentences
Even their body language says so much.

So if you find a someone
With whom silent you can be.
Actions speak louder than words
You'll have a lifetime guarantee.

My Second Childhood

I dread looking in the mirror
Facing stark reality
With saggy skin and crows feet
Where's the once younger me?

Don't judge me by these wrinkles
Or the shiny silver in my hair
And though my memory wanders
I've still so much to share.

Maturity is like a distant planet
Far removed from all that's young
But it's really all within my head
Whether my spring has sprung.

I just let it all hang out
What you get is what you see
Relax, enjoy, just be yourself
Set the child inside you free.

What fun; a second childhood
I will do better this time around
Not taking life so seriously
Enjoy the blessings that abound.

It's said youth is too important
Upon the young ones to waste
It takes mature inventive minds
To give life a proper embrace.

So regardless of outward me
Or the ways I've gone to 'pot'
Stand aside, I'm coming through
A sixty-eight year old TOT!

Long Living Rats

Eat blueberries
Inhale kale
And your arteries will stay clear.
Drink green tea
Soy is good
Then Alzheimers we need not fear.

Eating green veggies
And colorful fruit
Brings slow aging and brain repair.
Sip red wine
Enjoy dark chocolate
But you'll have to give up éclairs.

Today there is much confusion
As to methods that extend life.
Foods have been touted and oversold
Which can cause debate and strife.

Using proxy for sixty year old folk
Mole rats were tested for this info.
What do they have that we don't?
This plan I will have to forego.

To find the fountain of youth
Frequent fasting scientists advise.
But I enjoy three meals and snacks
So the above facts I will revise.

What's the fun in living long
If you're following rules for rats?
I certainly don't wish to wind up
A one hundred year old dingbat!

The Mature Youth

Is there any virtue to growing old
Since we've aced life's tests and matured?
Many value antique furniture and cars
Can't we be proud because we've endured?

Some feel we're second-class citizens
Our opinions and views count for nil.
But don't ignore all the knowledge stored
We're not yet over the 'proverbial hill'.

'Old age is not for sissies'
A truth that's often been said.
Just because our hair is gray
Doesn't mean our brain is dead.

The years roll by so quickly
Some folk become afraid and sad.
They battle daily to maintain youth
With Botox and facelifts the fad.

Today when youth is so revered
We face dual chins, jowls and pains.
Bodies sag due to earth's gravity
It's hard to recognize what remains.

We continue to learn from experience
But realize we'll never know it all.
And sometimes when our memory fails
Eventually our circuitry does recall.

Resolved is the search for life's meaning
Our answer is found in the Trinity.
God promised we'll never grow old
So our spirit forever young will be!

Not For Lunch

For many years an ideal marriage
With much love and little dissension
Then came the day that he retired
And life took on a new dimension -
For better, for worse, but not for lunch.

I can never answer the phone now
He gets it and listens in on my talks
I tell him, "Call your own friend."
"I've no one to talk to," he squawks -
For better, for worse, but not for lunch.

I tell him to get a hobby
I'm now his focus is his reply
He critiques every task I do
Which leads me to clarify -
For better, for worse, but not for lunch.

I still love the man I married
But where has that guy gone
What's left is a 'couch potato'
Who watches TV till dawn -
For better, for worse, but not for lunch.

Wedding vows should be amended
So wives would know what to expect
Then husbands would be informed
If preachers this phrase would inject -
For better, for worse, but not for lunch.

Urge your spouse to 'stay the course'
And remain among the employed
He will enjoy lunch with the guys
While you again can enjoy the void -
For better, for worse, but not more lunch.

Our 60th Reunion

We welcome the '47 Dragons
Blue and gold still runs in our veins.
The fond memories of Jefferson High
In our hearts will always remain.

Those once energetic young bodies
Have sagged heading due south.
Dim is our eyesight, memory is poor
Not many teeth left in our mouth.

Do you creak when you sit down
And utter a moan when you arise?
Is there a stiffness in your joints
A double vision thing in your eyes?

How often do you have to shout
"Speak up louder, I can't hear a thing?"
Your favorite foods you no longer eat
And Metamucil's praises you sing.

The city sidewalks are uphill now
We perspire and wheeze as we walk.
We seem to quickly run out of gas
So out of breath we can hardly talk.

Each stage of life has its rewards
On our travel to growing old.
With the silver in our hair and teeth
We're finally worth our weight in gold.

Yes, life's battles have taken their toll
Our boats sailed, our spring has sprung.
But in our minds, my fellow Dragons
We'll always be Forever Young!

The Good 'Ole Days'

What's good about the 'good ole days'
Growing up back in the dark ages?
There was no TV; imaginations flourished
Mental pictures surpassed those on stages.

The 'good ole days' were innocent…naïve
Boy meets girl, weds and has a family.
Children were disciplined for their own good
No indulgence given for each whining plea.

Marriage was a sacred covenant
That forever bound two as one.
Which, in turn, strengthened our nation
At that time, America was second to none.

We were kind and helpful to those we met
A living witness to the 'Golden Rule'.
Scant rudeness or road-rage present then
No horrible massacres at any school.

With all the progress and technology
How did our world go so awry?
While science can heal and prolong a life
Violence snuffs it out in the blink of an eye.

Sometimes the future seems hopeless
But there's still something we can do.
Lift high the cross of Jesus Christ
Through us, humanity can begin anew.

One by one, we can change the world
And wrestle it from its current phase.
Returning it to the status of old
So, TODAY, can be the 'good ole days'.

The Welcoming Committee

Hello, so nice to see you.
Welcome, how do you do?
Let me introduce myself
I'm Bertha Better Than You.

You'll have to sit down over here
That's Mary Moneybags pew.
Although very rich, she's stingy
Her tithe is running way past due.

We really have a saintly group
But sometimes the needy drop in.
And after all the glares they get
They leave and never come again.

Yes, gossip is a deadly sin
So I make an effort to try,
And pass on only the truth
Though not as juicy as a lie.

I do hope you'll feel at home
And want to join and be a part
Of Reverend Swansong's congregation
Though his sermons need a jumpstart.

Epilogue:

If you think that you'd fit in
With this group, shame on you
And should you be treated thusly
I'll tell you what to do...
Run as fast as the wind blows
Don't turn and look behind
For surely there's another church
Somewhere that you can find
Where you'll be treated kindly
With friendliness and self-worth
Which is what the Master had in mind
When He began His Kingdom on Earth.

The Parent Trap

When my folks said, "It's for your own good"
My eyes would glaze into a blank stare.
And told, "This will hurt me more than you"
While they swatted my bottom so bare.

No wonder kids think their parents are daft
Without one working cell in their brain.
Parents quickly proclaim their noble intent
But seem to be experts at inflicting pain.

It's then the thought process was begun
I'll not do or say those things to my child.
I'll be a more compassionate parent
No quick temper; my demeanor so mild.

Wonder of wonders, I have a child
Now I can try out my concepts so fine.
I will become an enlightened parent
No child will be better than mine.

His mother's good looks; his father's I.Q.
But he's born with a mind of his own.
I spout, "Don't do as I do, do as I say,
You can be the boss when you're grown."

I can't believe that's my voice I hear,
"For your own good, hurt me more than you."
I sound just like that parent of old,
And I've done what I said I'd not do.

So my child might have my same thoughts
When I was a young know it all lad.
And might change his mind and his rules
When as an adult, he becomes a dad.

So the moral of this treatise is
Youth think their parents aren't wise,
But by the time they become adults,
Suddenly, parents are geniuses in disguise.

HOLIDAYS

Rejoice in that day and leap for joy…

Luke 6: 23a

A New Year

A new year stretches before us
With many untold possibilities
A chance to begin anew
Facing our responsibilities.

Each day of the year is blank
Just waiting to be filled
With the choices we make
God's direction or our self-will.

God sent His only Son to us
So all sin might be erased
We cannot void our yesterdays
But this new year can be graced.

Before you choose acknowledge Christ
For He holds eternity in His scope
Then this year can be phenomenal
Filled with joy, His peace, and hope.

Resolutions

Most people make resolutions
When the New Year comes around
A new leaf must be turned over
As the Times Square Ball drops down.

The New Year is a time to reflect
And review the Old Year that's past
Assess the good things accomplished
All other things, rubbish to be cast.

Think positively and forgive
Eat healthy, exercise, lose weight
The resolutions list goes on and on
It's impossible to keep this mandate.

Who started this old tradition
Which inflicts enormous guilt?
Our resolve is quickly broken
Good intentions we often jilt.

Temptation rears its ugly head
Instantly commitment is gone
For the remaining new year's days
I give notice that I've withdrawn.

So now my yearly resolution is
Make NO New Year resolutions.
Officially I've recorded this in
The Jones Family Constitution.

New Opportunities

Last year's pages of life are filled
It's now time that they be turned
But first review events therein
Taking stock of what we've learned.

Much knowledge comes from experience
Choices made - some right, some wrong
Then we must strive to improve them
And become more dedicated and strong.

A brand new year has begun
We have blank pages to start
And fill with whatever we choose
The message we wish to impart.

We know who holds our future
And we daily surrender our will
So Christ's enduring promises
Through us, He can fulfill.

So carefully choose the entries
On each page of life you record
For there will be an accounting
Audited by Jesus Christ our Lord.

So pray we will be His witnesses
Throughout this brand new year
And might remain ever alert
For the day Christ will reappear.

True Love

The special day that's set aside
To honor love is almost here
Ads urge us to shop for gifts
For those we hold most dear.

Valentine's Day, a commercial gem
Selling flowers, candy and such
To express our true affections
And say, "I love you so much!"

But God, the creator of true love
Offers the gift that keeps on giving
By sending His Son to die on a cross
To provide us with eternal living.

No greater love than Christ
Could any one of us know
He asks that we pass it on
Never interrupting its flow.

So when we honor our Valentines
Recall by whom we were shown
How to love with heart and soul
And keep our Lord enthroned.

Forty Days

The time for Lent has begun
Heed its deep spiritual meaning
Forty days hence we will observe
Christ's sacrifice for our redeeming.

In the wilderness for forty days
Satan's temptations Christ resisted
Though human, He is the Son of God
And for this express job He enlisted.

When we can identify as His child
We have access to Christ's power
Not just for the forty days of Lent
But daily…minute by minute…
Hour by hour.

God's Plan

How amazing is His love
So great Christ's sacrifice
As He hung dying on the cross
Soldiers rolled their dice.

Gambling for the clothes Christ wore
A souvenir from the King of the Jews
He still had clothes of righteousness
Christ's arising was good news.

Weeping Mary watched in anguish
The pain her firstborn son endured
Knowing God's plan had come to pass
So Eternal Life could be assured.

His body lay in a dark dank tomb
But wasn't there on the third day
Believers rejoiced; Rome doubted
As always God had the final say.

Still today we make our plans
God laughs for they're not His own
He holds us safely in His arms
And forever reigns on His throne.

Deny Him Not

If you'd been outside the palace
Amidst that large unruly throng
And heard Pilate question Jesus
Would you have stood firm and strong?

Then shouted without hesitation,
"He's blameless, sin free, let Him go!"
Or like Judas and Peter betray Him
And then, thrice, hear the cock crow.

Running away in fear and confusion
Crushed with self-loathing and shame
Instead of being 'the rock' Christ chose
Denied knowing the Savior's name.

We've all walked that path to Calvary
Also hammered a nail in His cross
We've silently witnessed injustice
And took our place with the dross.

But because Jesus so loves us
He died on that hill in our place
And holds out His nail-scarred hands
Which covers our sins with His grace.

If we repent and claim Him as Savior
And choose to follow His way
We then will receive Eternal Life
 Please answer His call, don't delay.

The Shouts

Shouts of "Hosanna" rang out
When Jesus entered Jerusalem
The people rejoiced, waving palms
Though Christ they would later condemn.

The Pharisees sought to trap him
And questioned Christ's authority
While disciples ate the Last Supper
Judas betrayed Christ for a small fee.

Shouts of "Crucify him" were heard
Christ was tried; Barabbas set free
Crowned with thorns Christ hung on a cross
His blood covered our sins on Calvary.

Christ shouted, "Father forgive them"
Even then, for all, did intercede
Then weakly He said, "It is finished."
Finally over, this dastardly deed.

The disciples dispersed in fear
Thinking God's plan had gone awry
For still they did not understand
Christ's mission was not just to die.

Shouts of "He is risen" were heard
Christ was gone when the women came
He was resurrected three days after death
Fulfilling scripture that had been proclaimed.

Christ appeared to his disciples again.
Explaining the path that lay ahead
They were empowered by his presence
And listened intently to what Jesus said.

"Make disciples of every nation
In the name of Father, Spirit and Son
And I will remain with you always
My earthly kingdom has now begun."

At the last shout of "Hallelujah"
Christ ascended but His Spirit remains
In our hearts, air we breathe, beauty seen
Over all the whole universe He reigns.

After Easter

After all the lilies have wilted
The Resurrection songs put away
Do we return to life as usual
As if there'd been no Easter day?

Garments are wrinkled and faded
Gone from our face is the glow
We resume our daily routines
As if nothing to Jesus we owe.

Stilled are the joyful hosannas
No trumpets blast forth with joy
Again consumed by earthly cares
As if Mary had borne no boy.

Near Emmaus they knew Him not
But we can see Christ sans disguise
Which makes each glorious day Easter
If we claim Him we too, shall arise.

Resurrection Proclaimed

What had begun in the manger
Came to fruition at last
The time for Jesus had come
Just as the prophets had forecast.

Jesus came to teach us God's truth
About the world and what it could be
To strike a holy spark within us
So we'd perceive His Divinity.

Christ offered us God's treasure
The amazing gift of Eternal Life
Though many believed his teachings
Others stayed mired in sinful strife.

His disciples thought He'd banish Rome
Then rich and powerful they would be
But the Pharisees conspired with Judas
Captured and jailed the innocent of Galilee.

Beaten, bloodied, unjustly sentenced to die
Christ carried a cross; as the crowd jeered
The soldiers drove nails and crucified Him
Still Christ prayed for them as death neared.

His body was buried in a dank tomb
Which was empty on the third day
His resurrection was proclaimed to all
Proving death could not keep its prey.

Still we tell the profound Easter story
For even now many don't understand
That only through Christ's love and grace
Can we inherit the kingdom God planned.

Salute To Moms

Those who had mothers
That loved them dearly
Should thank the Lord each day
For kindness and love
Daily encouragement
Being taught to kneel and pray.

She read them stories
Cared for all needs
A five-star mother for sure
She cleaned, cooked meals
Consoled when ill
For each problem she had the cure.

As her children matured
She gave them wings
So they'd be the best they could be
They'd choose their own path
With no guilt imposed
She'd remain their proud trustee.

If this wasn't your life
Accept my regrets
But for you there's another route
Be the kind of Mom
You wished you'd had
And you'll deserve a 21 gun salute.

Oh, but lucky you
If this was your life
I'm sure you have no remorse
You've raised your brood
The same way you were
As your mother's rules you endorsed.

Memorial Day

Memorial Day honors the valor and courage
Of the many brave souls under the sod
With pride they answered America's call
For them we offer grateful prayers to God.

Our nation's flag flies at half-mast
As we recall those who fought and died
To preserve America's many freedoms
We salute you; our hearts swell with pride.

Facing danger they paid the price
To keep our country's citizens free
So offer a prayer and don't forget
Who bought freedom for you and me.

Heroes still fight tyranny today
O'er our land the Stars and Stripes wave
Insuring that this great country of ours
Will remain home of the free and the brave.

Father of All Fathers

Almighty Father of all Fathers
Bless all dads here below
May they follow your example
With tenderness their love bestow.

Children learn by what they see
So may fathers emulate you
And be mindful of their image
Faithful, steadfast and true.

As they guide and protect their children
Jesus' compassion may they display
And should they harbor any flaws
Remind them 'straight is the way'.

If said,"Do as I say, not as I do,"
To youth, that won't make the grade
Callous, hard-hearted, insensitive
Will make their fatherhood a charade.

May they value their importance
Of young lives within their care
And mirror your love and devotion
Heavenly Father, this is our prayer.

Thanksgiving

We view the world with eyes aware
Noting things we take for granted
We often ignore the simple joys
Seeming jaded and disenchanted.

Our lives have become so busy, Lord
We often forget to praise or thank you
For the many blessings you provide us
Our gratitude is greatly overdue.

God we thank you for your love
Also that of friends and family
Thanks for food, homes, health
That we live in a land that's free.

We have such great abundance
And realize you are its source
If all your gifts to us were listed
It would be longer than this discourse.

Suffice to say we are thankful
The blessing of life we appreciate
We could never say thank you enough
For being our loving Advocate.

Giving Thanks

'Enter His gates with Thanksgiving
And into His courts with praise'
Countless blessings God bestows
To enhance our earthly days.

We thank the Lord for salvation
The gift of undeserved grace
Whereby we have become heirs
Of that glorious Holy place.

We thank Him for our loved ones
Both family and dear friends
He supplies our daily needs
Our all on the Lord depends.

We praise Christ for the lessons
That love alone can teach
And pray we will pass them on
To those He wishes to reach.

Thank Christ for the Holy Spirit
Whose presence gives us strength
To face the trials of the world
With a future of endless length.

So we thank the Lord and praise Him
For reaching out to such as we
May we remain His witnesses
And be all He would have us be.

Son of God

We celebrate Christmas joyously
Not understanding all that took place
Our God…omnipotent…all powerful
He came to earth to share our space.

But God had a plan for His Son
Involving all of us…everyone
Whereby the world could be saved
By acknowledging Christ as God's Son.

He was a baby as we were
And became part of a family
Things that hurt us hurt Him too
But Christ forgives quicker than we.

This Son of God died on a cross
His blood would remove every stain
And those who accept Him as Savior
Everlasting life we will then gain.

There Is Room

Three Wisemen journeyed
To follow a bright star
Over two thousand years ago.
They were noble and wise
But Scriptures revealed
Further truth they wanted to know.

A birth in a stable,
The Holy One came
To save all humanity.
And now we can sing
"Come into my heart, Lord,
There's room in my heart for Thee."

We, like the Wisemen
Must retrace the steps
That many seekers have trod.
Not back to Bethlehem
But to our heart's door
Opened wide to Christ, Son of God.

Though busy our lives
Christ still needs to know
That He is our Savior and King.
And still holds the key
To that room in our hearts
And is the Lord of everything.

In Our Midst

Are there still shepherds in our midst
Who are willing to follow Christ's star
Laying aside all worldly things
Using Christ as their exemplar?

Are there still Magi in our midst
Who realize they know not all
Wanting to lay gifts at His feet
And worship this Babe so small?

Are there still sinners in our midst
Whom the Word hasn't been shared
They stumble about in deep darkness
For Heaven their souls aren't prepared?

Are we still worshipping that Babe
Languishing quietly in that manger
Never mentally moving from that scene
Nor claiming the adult Christ as Savior?

Christ, God's Son, died for our sins
And deserves our love and dedication.
Not just at Christmas but every day
For He gave us the gift of salvation.

God's Christmas Gift

Long ago in Bethlehem
God presented us a gift
Jesus Christ – Prince of Peace
Who came to rescue those adrift.

Still today many are afraid
God's precious gift to accept
They feel unworthy of His love
Due to commandments unkept.

Some unwrap it so carefully
Saving the paper and the bows
They don't receive the full blessing
That this gift on them bestows.

Others tear into it so quickly
With much delight they respond
Eager to enjoy its contents
To the gift, they instantly bond.

Praise God for His marvelous gift
That frees us from sin and death
We now face eternity with Christ
Who lovingly wrote our bequest.

Yes, Christmas is a time for gifts
But we are usually the receiver
Now it's time to reciprocate, so…
Gift your heart to God as a believer.

A Holy Event

On the most holy of nights
A wondrous miracle took place
A small Baby came to earth
To share His love and grace.

Did this take place in a palace?
No, in a stable was His birth
Royal vestments? No, swaddling clothes
Clothed this Baby of infinite worth.

What had been prophesied long ago
In this Child had now come to be
The bright star shining on this scene
Led shepherds and three Magi to see.

What the future held they knew not
As they knelt and worshiped in awe
Quietly Mary watched, then shivered
As the shadow of a cross she saw.

This blessed Babe, Mary, Joseph, us
All part of God's salvation plan
Whereby Christ would die on a cross
To negate all the sins of man.

From beginning to end this treatise tells
That Christ's love is ours if we choose
So go and share this Holy Event
And the saving grace of God's good news.

Affluenza

Department stores are ready
Before a chill is in the air
Displaying Christmas goodies
So we'll spend like millionaires.

The tree is trimmed and ready
The gifts wrapped and toys assembled
But when I looked at all the 'stuff'
Suddenly it seemed I trembled.

Excess truly clutters our lives
A long list of things we claim
It seems we're never satisfied
Getting more is our constant aim.

For some malls are their church
As affluenza takes its greedy toll
Buying becomes a sacrament
When indulgence gains control.

Affluenza is a worldly disease
Which approves the desire for stuff
An addiction for needless things
Must have them; Can't get enough.

But happiness doesn't come in a box
The cure for affluenza I've found
Be content with what you have
With true wealth you will abound.

Would We?

If we had lived during Bible times
Would we have sensed the godly nature
Of this holy infant King born in a manger
Gifted with frankincense and myrrh?

Eagerly awaiting the Messiah
Jesus, the Son, would we have known
Or would we have joined the noisy crowd
And perhaps, have hurled a stone?

The Rabbi who enthralled us
We followed from town to town
His teachings touched our hearts
Could we then have let Him down?

Would we have gone to Gethsemane
To pray with Him but fall asleep
Could we have joined the Pharisees
Betray this sinless One, then weep?

Would we have carried His heavy cross
Or driven nails in it as Christ hung
Afraid as day turned dark as night
The silver pieces would we have flung?

In anguished sorrow would we confess
This monstrous sin that had been done
Or acknowledging Christ as Savior
Could He then our souls have won?

Though we're living in the 'here and now'
We're still faced with the same decision
Will you accept Christ today as Savior
And share His glorious eternal vision?

God's Holy Heir

The Word became flesh
And dwelt among us
On that first Christmas Day
Son of Mary and God
The Holy Child slept
Through the night on a bed of hay.

The Babe didn't awaken
As the bright star shone
Its beams on God's Holy Heir
Old Scripture fulfilled
Earth's Kingdom began
In a dark stable with no fanfare.

Still Baby Jesus slept
As the shepherds came
To see what angels did proclaim
Their fear was dissolved
When they gazed at Christ
Knowing they'd never be the same.

The Wisemen had seen
And followed the star
Seeking the King who'd been foretold
And as the Babe dozed
They presented their gifts
Myrrh, frankincense and precious gold.

No wisemen we
With costly gifts
But God in His mercy and grace
Provided the way
To Eternal Life
By suffering in our place.

When as an adult
Christ taught God's Word
And turned the world upside down
He died on a cross
To blot out our sins
And fit us for Eternity's crown.

Christmas Each Day

Why don't we celebrate Christmas
Each day of every year
Showing kindness and compassion
To those both far and near?

If we could bottle up the glow
From the joy of anticipation
And prescribe a spoonful every day
A change would sweep our nation!

Our spirits grow more mellow
When Advent season comes around
We're more generous and helpful
To needy ones whom life has bound.

We delight in helping others
Thus, practicing brotherly love
We see a bit of Heaven on earth
A preview of what awaits us above.

Our Father sees and is well pleased
When we witness and do our part
To further His earthly kingdom
Keeping Christmas each day in our heart.

Yes, love came down at Christmas
With angelic refrains and glory
His joy and grace overwhelms us
As we recall the wondrous story.

So honor our Lord with thanks and praise
Always adore and make Him a part
Of your life by always striving
To keep Christmas each day in your heart.

What Is Christmas?

Christmas is quickly approaching
So many things to be done
Trim the tree, address the cards
I dare not forget even one.

I carefully check my gift list
Noting items, color and size
Hoping that the choices I make
Brings much joy to their eyes.

Baking, cooking, wrapping gifts
All this busyness has me stressed
Belatedly, ashamed, I sadly realize
I've forgotten the most important guest.

The one who brought 'Joy to the World'
Who caused the angel chorus to sing
The Babe who laid in a manger of hay
JESUS CHRIST…the King of Kings.

There would be no reason to rejoice
Without the birth of God's Son
He makes Christmas, 'Christmas'
Not these tasks we think must be done.

So when you see those twinkling lights
Remember, He's the 'Light of the World'
May your presents recall His priceless gift
Salvation through Him was unfurled.

What gift is worthy for such a King
Frankincense, myrrh, or gold so grand?
No, just the fact that you claim Him as Lord
And present Him your heart in His hand.

Two Views of Christmas

To the Worldly - Christmas Means:

Spending too much for presents
Wrapping gifts, trimming the tree
Baking, cooking till midnight
Why am I the only one on K.P.?

Addressing cards, writing notes
The list gets longer each year
Decorating the house and yard
Hurry, the day is almost here.

The meal that took hours, was gone in a flash
Bows, paper strewn, gifts to be exchanged
How quickly that warm feeling dissolves
All the stress leaves me feeling deranged.

To the Christian - Christmas Means:

Our Lord Jesus was born on this day
To bring us salvation He came
Though sinless, Christ died on a cross
 And the world would never be the same.

Those who belong to Christ
Act as servants to those they meet
Dedicating every deed to Him
And lay their gifts at His feet.

So consider the truth of this day
Its worth exceeds all treasure known
For believers look forward to Eternity
As Christ forever cares for His own.

ABOUT JO ANN

Jo Ann Jones is a lifetime resident of Tampa, Florida. Even as a youngster she was creative and wrote stories to amuse the children in her large family. Jo Ann also enjoyed singing solos in the church choir. In high school she wrote articles and stories for her high school newspaper.

At a retreat, in her late teens, she accepted Christ as her Savior. Jo Ann began composing poems which she shared with family, friends and fellow church members. As her faith grew, she began writing poems of a personal nature touching on happy and sad events we each encounter throughout life.

Though many may see the same event, each person might be affected in a different way. Within this book she has shared her innermost thoughts, freely expressing herself, and hopefully, offering her own insight to others.

www.ingramcontent.com/pod-product-compliance
Lightning Source LLC
Chambersburg PA
CBHW070640050426
42451CB00008B/239